YOUR KNOWLEDGE HAS VALUE

- We will publish your bachelor's and master's thesis, essays and papers

- Your own eBook and book - sold worldwide in all relevant shops

- Earn money with each sale

Upload your text at www.GRIN.com
and publish for free

Bibliographic information published by the German National Library:

The German National Library lists this publication in the National Bibliography; detailed bibliographic data are available on the Internet at http://dnb.dnb.de .

This book is copyright material and must not be copied, reproduced, transferred, distributed, leased, licensed or publicly performed or used in any way except as specifically permitted in writing by the publishers, as allowed under the terms and conditions under which it was purchased or as strictly permitted by applicable copyright law. Any unauthorized distribution or use of this text may be a direct infringement of the author s and publisher s rights and those responsible may be liable in law accordingly.

Imprint:

Copyright © 2017 GRIN Verlag, Open Publishing GmbH
Print and binding: Books on Demand GmbH, Norderstedt Germany
ISBN: 9783668433564

This book at GRIN:

http://www.grin.com/en/e-book/358959/gabriel-s-artistic-development-in-the-face-of-death-in-james-joyce-s-short

Nadine Fischer

Gabriel's Artistic Development in the Face of Death in James Joyce's Short Story "The Dead"

GRIN Publishing

GRIN - Your knowledge has value

Since its foundation in 1998, GRIN has specialized in publishing academic texts by students, college teachers and other academics as e-book and printed book. The website www.grin.com is an ideal platform for presenting term papers, final papers, scientific essays, dissertations and specialist books.

Visit us on the internet:

http://www.grin.com/

http://www.facebook.com/grincom

http://www.twitter.com/grin_com

Ludwig-Maximilians-Universität München

Department of English Studies

Winter Semester 2016/17

The aesthetics of modernist fiction: Joyce, Woolf and Faulkner

Gabriel's Artistic Development in the Face of Death in James Joyce's Short Story *The Dead*

Nadine Fischer

Germanistische Literaturwissenschaft M.A.

First Semester

Table of Contents

1. INTRODUCTION 3

2. ALLUSIONS TO DEATH 4

3. GABRIEL BEFORE BECOMING AN ARTIST 7

4. THE TURNING POINT 11

5. THE ULTIMATE INSIGHT 13

6. CONCLUSION 17

REFERENCES 18

Primary Sources 18

Secondary Sources 18

1. Introduction

Reading essays on James Joyce's short story *The Dead*, one is immediately confronted with the most different interpretations of its end as it is very different from the rest of the text and can even be seen as poetic. Apparently Gabriel's epiphany is of prime importance to the readers of James Joyce. This term paper shall answer the question why this is the case. Therefore it is necessary to comprehend the extreme development of Gabriel within the story. This work claims that Gabriel, rather self-centred at the beginning, develops into an understanding artist towards the end of the story when he is somehow challenged by the dead after his wife's revelation. Eco states that "all of Joyce's works might be understood as a continuous discussion of their own artistic procedure" (Eco 2007: 329) and I think this is also the case in *The Dead*. As the title of the short story already reveals, death plays a huge role in the text, especially when causing Gabriel's final enlightenment. To prove this thesis, first of all allusions to death in the text shall be found and interpreted as they function as framework for the gloomy core revealed at the end and thereby pave the way to Gabriel's aesthetic development. Then the main character shall be examined on his artistic premises before the turning point signifies a change in his aesthetic views. In the last chapter Gabriel's transformation into an artist shall be elucidated more precisely with an emphasis put on his changing reception of the omnipresent snow transferring into a poetical symbol of death. The snow motive connects art and death and therefore anticipates the aesthetic transformation in the views of the main character towards the much discussed end of the short story. This essay lays weight on a close contemplation of the short story, based on Fishelov's founded observation:

> The fact that no dramatic event takes place during the present story time, and the fact that the story focuses on Gabriel's inner world, together with the poetic qualities of the text [...] all encourage the reader to further concentrate on minute textual details and on small emotional and semantic nuances, characteristics that are traditionally associated with lyric poetry. (Fishelov 2013/2014: 263)

The final conclusion will summarize the most important insights and give some indication on whether the initial hypothesis can be validated or not.

2. Allusions to death

The most obvious reference to death can be found in the title of James Joyce's short story which is called *The Dead*. The story delivers what the title promises, although more modest at the beginning. The first word of the text is "Lily" (Joyce 1971: 7) for example, which is not only the name of the caretaker's daughter, but also of a flower most commonly associated with funerals and thus the beginning already introduces mortality as one of the most prominent topics of the story.

Furthermore the reader learns also on the first page that the whole setting of the story – the annual dance of the Morkan's in their "dark, gaunt house on Usher's Island" (Joyce 1971: 7) – is born out of the death of a family member. The sombre framework casts a shadow on the whole storyline and implies that the superficial seeming actions have a further meaning.

Another interesting point is, how the people who are joining the party are described: the two aunts of Gabriel as "grey" and "feeble" with "mirthless eyes" (Joyce 1971: 8, 11, 12), Lily although in the bloom of youth as "slim" and "pale" (Joyce 1971: 9) and Mrs Malins as "a stout, feeble old woman with white hair" (Joyce 1971: 22). Considering these moribund descriptions, Jones definitely has a point in stating that "Time lays as heavily upon them as the snow accumulating outside during the course of the night" (Jones 2000: 110). The meaning of the omnipresent snow will be further clarified in the last chapter. With that said it is no wonder that the annual dance often is interpreted as a party of deceased. In my opinion this assertion is not sustainable as there is no further evidence for it. But I do consent to Merino who claims that James Joyce's *The Dead* is "[e]pitomizing notions of paralysis, exile or return to the origin" (Merino 2016: 133).

Paralysis plays also a role in the recurring event of the party with its frozen procedures repeating every year: "[f]or years and years it had gone off in splendid style, as long as anyone could remember" (Joyce 1971: 7). Obviously nothing ever changes in the setting of the annual dance which reminds of the constancy of death. So it is all the more striking that the main character Gabriel is able to overcome this perpetual stagnation which shall be elucidated in the following chapters.

As the party takes place in winter it is not surprising that it is very cold outside. It is however remarkable how often and how drastically the frostily weather is addressed in the text: "she must be perished alive", "Gretta caught a dreadful cold", "Mrs Malins will get her death of cold", or "everybody has colds" (Joyce 1971: 9, 12, 39, 44). The weather conditions attack the characters in the story by affecting their health. Serious sickness seems to be a ubiquitous threat that comes consistently to the fore and reminds us of our evanescence.

Another important point is that transience invades the security of the superficial party small talk several times. The harmless conversation about the bracing air in Mount Melleray and the hospitality of the local monks turns unexpectedly towards mortality as one of the guests wonders why the monks sleep in coffins: "'The coffin', said Mary Jane, 'is to remind them of their last end" (Joyce 1971: 34). The topic is not really fit for the occasion and the visitors feel noticeably uneasy by the remembrance of death: "As the subject had grown lugubrious it was buried in a silence of the table" (Joyce 1971: 34). A really targeting metaphor as the dead are also buried in coffins. This shows that the guests can keep silence about this precarious topic but nonetheless death is inevitably present in the background all the time.

It is also noticeable that the focus of attention shifts from Lilly to Gabriel's thoughts when he finally arrives. Why not beginning the story with the focus on Gabriel at the party? Jones explains the tardiness of the main character and the fear of his aunts that another guest might arrive drunk with their importance for an anticipation of the story's major themes: "In these couple of sentences, Joyce throws into the air the first balls that he will be juggling throughout the story: absence, longing for arrival, and forces that cannot be controlled" (Jones 2000: 110). Gabriel also uses an extraordinary expression to justify their delay when stating that his wife Gretta "takes three mortal hours to dress herself" (Joyce 1971: 8). Almost subconsciously he seems to be somehow occupied with decease already at the beginning of the story. Furthermore military vocabulary is used frequently in the apparently inappropriate context of the party and thus also brings transience to the fore subconsciously (Winston 2004: 122-132). Later when contemplating a photograph of his departed mother, Gabriel also reflects about "her last long illness" (Joyce 1971: 19). And even in his speech he feels urged to remind the attendants of "those dead and gone great ones whose fame the world will not willingly let die" and of "absent faces that we miss here tonight" (Joyce 1971: 36). Although being aware of the audience's uncomfortableness with the topic of death and although claiming that he "will not linger on the past", Gabriel is resolved to contaminate the seemingly carefree atmosphere of the party with "such sad memories" (Joyce 1971: 37). Gabriel's first reflections about mortality are more of superficial nature but one can nonetheless already anticipate that the main character is more willing to face the sombre subject of transience than the other party guests. How this relation between Gabriel and death intensifies throughout the short story shall be explained in the following chapters.

3. Gabriel before becoming an Artist

Gabriel is described as "stout, tallish young man"(Joyce 1971: 10) which conveys a rather formidable effect at first. But opposing to this first impression the main character is further presented as agitable, sensitive and unsettled:

> The high colour of his cheeks pushed upwards even his forehead, where it scattered itself in a few formless patches of pale red; and on his hairless face there scintillated restlessly the polished lenses and the bright gilt rims of the glasses which screened his delicate and restless eyes. (Joyce 1971: 10).

The fact that the word "restless" is used two times in one sentence is really conspicuous and apparently characteristic for Gabriel as a master stylist like James Joyce will probably not have used the same expression twice by accident. It signalizes that Gabriel has obviously not yet been arrived in his life, an impression that will even intensify during the course of the evening. This disruption in the characterization of Gabriel already augurs the multilayeredness of his personality that will especially emerge at the end of the story. Jones states aptly: "Gabriel is at a distance from us, he will see everything in the story then from behind glass, which also makes him difficult to be seen directly." (Jones 2000: 111) But this distance which will later constitute Gabriel's perception of the world is clearly lacking at the beginning of the story. We learn for instance that the main character is obviously not very skilful in dealing with other people as we can see right at the outset. He has a very uncomfortable encounter with the caretaker's daughter Lily and reacts anything but clinical to it: "Gabriel coloured, as if he felt he had made a mistake, and, without looking at her, kicked off his goloshes and flicked actively with his muffler at his patent leather-shoes" (Joyce 1971: 10). Gabriel's reaction to Lily's back answer resembles the tantrum of a little child and to cover his shame he treats Lily contemptuous, "waving his hand to her in deprecation" (Joyce 1971: 10). But still he is "discomposed by the girl's bitter and sudden retort" (Joyce 1971: 10) which even leads him to question his well-prepared speech:

> He would only make himself ridiculous by quoting poetry to them which they could not understand. They would think that he was airing his superior education. He would fail with them just as he had failed with the girl in the pantry. He had taken up a wrong tone. His whole speech was a mistake from first to last, an utter failure. (Joyce 1971: 11)

This reflection about tone and culture-bound differences in language reminds of the always scrutinizing Stephen in James Joyce's partly biographical novel *A Portrait of the Artist as a Young Man*: "His language, so familiar and so foreign, will always be for me an acquired speech. I have not made or accepted its words" (Joyce 2000: 159). This parallel to Stephen who will develop into an artist throughout the novel implies that there is also an aesthetic potential in Gabriel which only has to be released.

In regard of Gabriel's relationship to art it is important to refer to his reception of it on the one hand and to his own creative work on the other. Considering the first aspect it is illuminating to take a closer look on how Gabriel perceives the academy piece that Mary Jane plays on the piano: "He liked music, but the piece she was playing had no melody for him and he doubted whether it had any melody for the other listeners" (Joyce 1971: 18). This shows that Gabriel has no interest in "higher" forms of art. He likes music in general as anybody probably does, but the aesthetic of complex artistry is not accessible to him. He also mentions that "his mother had had no musical talent" (Joyce 1971: 18) and this assertion presumably also applies to him. But then after reflecting about his deceased mother, her "sullen opposition to his marriage" and "her last long illness" he all of a sudden gets a certain feeling for the music and intuits the piano piece will be over soon: "He knew that Mary Jane must be near the end of her piece, for she was playing again the opening melody with runs of scales after every bar, and while he waited for the end the resentment died down in his heart" (Joyce 1971: 19). Apparently after reflecting about death, the music even has a cathartic effect on him as he distances himself from his feelings. Like his mother after her long disease his negative emotions die down in his heart. This is the first sign that art and death are connected in a way and that Gabriel's aesthetic attitude changes in the eye of death.

But this distance towards his feelings does not last long as the awareness of transience in form of some short reflection about passed away relatives does not have a permanent impact obviously. Shortly after this passage Gabriel's confidence is shaken by Miss Ivors accusing him of being a "West Briton" for writing a literary column for "The Daily Express". So we learn that Gabriel is an author in a way though he is not creating his own literary works but rather reflecting about the writing of others. He is more of a passionate reader than a writer himself: "He loved to feel the covers and turn over the pages of newly printed books" (Joyce 1971: 20). Moreover Gabriel holds the opinion that "literature [is] above politics" (Joyce 1971: 20), although he does not proclaim his aesthetic views – he buries them in silence just like the party guests did with the gloomy topic before. One senses that Gabriel wants to stay uncontaminated which is also symbolized by his obsession with galoshes: "It reminds [...] of the galoshes; Gabriel takes care to not be in direct contact with the elements, inside or outside of himself" (Jones 2000: 111). He wants to be dissociated from the impact of others on his unsteady self-confidence as it is already clarified in his perceived sophisticated superiority over the other guests, but he is not able to keep himself from being affected by them: "'O, to tell you the truth', retorted Gabriel suddenly, 'I'm sick of my own country, sick of it!'" (Joyce 1971: 22). This aversion of his home country Ireland reminds once more of Stephen in *A Portrait of the Artist as a Young Man*: "I will not serve that in which I no longer believe whether it call itself my home, my fatherland or my church: and I will try to express myself in some mode of life or art as freely as I can" (Joyce 2000: 208).

After this second unpleasant encounter Gabriel once more begins to reflect about his speech and wishes himself away from the party. "How pleasant it would be to walk out alone, first along by the river and then through the park! [...] How much more pleasant it would be there than at the supper-table!" (Joyce 1971: 24). After this short mental escape Gabriel's thoughts return back to his speech: "He ran over the headings of his speech [...] He repeated to himself a phrase he had written in his review: 'One feels that one is listening to a thought-tormented music'" (Joyce: 1971: 24). Gabriel really is thought-tormented in point of fact. He does not seem able to keep his eagerly anticipated distance, instead he cannot stop reflecting about what others might think of him or of his speech. Gabriel definitely lacks self-assurance and confidence in his gift for languages. Benbida summarizes this issue concisely: "He is a man of words without the ability to communicate; he is frustrated in expressing himself" (Benbida 2013: 46). This diagnosis also consolidates in the preliminary sentences of Gabriel's speech:

> It has fallen to my lot this evening, as in years past, to perform a very pleasing task, but a task for which I am afraid my poor powers as a speaker are all too inadequate. [...] I endeavour to express to you in words what my feelings are on this occasion. (Joyce 1971: 35)

This is apparently a falsehood as Gabriel has well-conceived his speech several times from first to last beforehand so that he does not reveal his sincere and spontaneous sentiments. Besides his prevalent feeling has been the longing for escapade so far which he of course does not mention in his oration. Comparing his decrepit aunts to the graces is mere hypocrisy when shortly before referring to them as "two ignorant old women" (Joyce 1971: 25). Gabriel therefor cannot be considered yet as an artist as he is superficial and dishonest in his speech and not self-creating when writing reviews.

4. The Turning Point

This changes when Gabriel sees Gretta listening to "The Lass of Aughrim". He cannot hear the song himself but he nonetheless "does deeply experience her listening" (Jones 2000: 113). Gabriel does not even recognize his wife at first, both of them are standing in the shadow but are separated from each other:

> He stood still in the gloom of the hall, trying to catch the air that the voice was singing and gazing up at his wife. There was grace and mystery in her attitude as if she were a symbol of something. He asked himself what is a woman standing on the stairs in the shadow, listening to distant music, a symbol of. If he were a painter he would paint her in that attitude. Her blue felt hat would show off the bronze of her hair against the darkness and the dark panels of her skirt would show off the light ones. *Distant Music* he would call the picture if he were a painter. (Joyce 1971: 43)

This scene arises the impression that "he worships a frozen effigy of his wife, whom he imagines as a painting" (Munich 1984: 182) and thus resembles some kind of "reversed" Pygmalion (Ovid 2011: 324-326) who aestheticizes his vivid wife into a lifeless statue in his thoughts which obviously inspires him. Moreover, his reflection about symbolism already signifies that Gabriel develops into an Artist and reminds once again of Stephen's aesthetic contemplations of the meaning of metaphors in *A Portrait of the Artist as a Young Man*: "How could a woman be a tower of ivory or a house of gold?" (Joyce 2000: 28). But Stephen answers his questions in the following whereas Gabriel is not able to find a solution for his artistic considerations yet:

> Here Gabriel is the active, if unsuccessful, symbol searcher; he perceives his very flesh and blood wife as an aesthetic object. Although he asks what she is a symbol of, we know that he doesn't know the answer, he doesn't really know what spiritual quality is embodied in her attitude of 'grace and mystery' (Morrissey 1988: 26)

That is because he tries to see things from a painter's perspective which is obviously the wrong art form as Gabriel is de facto a writer. He gets inspired by his wife's attitude with a "sudden tide of joy [...] leaping out of his heart" (Joyce 1971: 45). Gabriel who has been trying to be emotionally distanced the whole evening suddenly lets himself getting overwhelmed by his feelings: "The blood went bounding along his veins and the thoughts went rioting through his brain, proud, joyful, tender, valorous" (Joyce 1971: 46). Everything seems intensified, enforced by the twice used simile: "Moments of their secret life together burst like stars upon his memory" (Joyce 1971: 46). From now on Gabriel's thoughts are full of romantic stylistic devices which brings him nearer to a poet:

> A wave of yet more tender joy escaped from his heart and went coursing in warm flood along his arteries. Like the tender fire of stars moments of their life together, that no one knew of or would ever know of, broke upon and illuminated his memory (Joyce 1971: 47).

Furthermore Gabriel states that "[t]heir children, his writing, her household cares had not quenched all their souls' tender fire" (Joyce 1971: 47). Mentioning "his writing" in the same breath with other obligations, shows once more that his journalistic task is rather a job than artwork to him. But now love letters he once had written for his wife are appearing in his mind "[l]ike distant music" (Joyce 1971: 47) which points out again where this fulcrum in his artistic attitude derives its origin from. Nevertheless all these reflections inspired by love and lust are in a way poetic but also seem very sugary and exaggerated. "'The Lass of Aughrim' like the narration of 'The Dead' is art: and art does not speak the truth of social reality" (Norris 1989: 495). Gabriel also seems to flee his own social reality by aestheticizing his relationship: "he felt that they had escaped from their lives and duties, escaped from home and friends and run away together with wild and radiant hearts to a new adventure" (Joyce 1971: 48). He thinks he finally managed to get away from it all but he is mistaken at this point. It is just a tempting illusion which will be destroyed all the more cruelly by Gretta's following revelation.

5. The Ultimate Insight

Gretta admits that before marrying Gabriel there has been a boy called Michael Furey in her life who had loved her and even had died for her. Gabriel feels humiliated by this boy from the gasworks: "While he had been full of memories of their secret life together, full of tenderness and joy she had been comparing him in her mind with another" (Joyce 1971: 52). This extreme discrepancy between their moods and thoughts makes Gabriel's whole life appear in a different light. Gretta's revelation shocks him and provokes a sudden moment of self-recognition in Gabriel resulting in a devastating conclusion:

> A shameful consciousness of his own person assailed him. He saw himself as a ludicrous figure, acting as a pennyboy for his aunts, a nervous, well-meaning sentimentalist, orating to vulgarians and idealizing his own clownish lusts, the pitiable fatuous fellow he had caught a glimpse of in the mirror. (Joyce 1971: 52-53).

Gabriel even senses he is challenged by the dead who have a certain power he cannot overcome at first: "A vague terror seized Gabriel [...], as if, at that hour when he had hoped to triumph, some impalpable and vindictive being was coming against him, gathering forces against him in its vague world" (Joyce 1971: 53). But he is able to overcome his shock. He suddenly feels "a strange, friendly pity" for Gretta and "wondered at his riot of emotions of an hour before" (Joyce 1971: 55). Gabriel like after listening to Mary Jane's academic peace and reflecting about the deceased also experiences a kind of catharsis after this much more intense encounter with the dead. "Gabriel's epiphany manifests Joyce's fundamental belief that true, objective perception will lead to true, objective sympathy" (Loomis 1960: 149). This objective perception liberates him from his egoism and enables him to leave his own self-centred world. He is not caught up in his emotions anymore and finally reaches his long desiderated distance which is according to Stephen's aesthetics in *A portrait of the Artist as a Young Man* characteristic for an artist: "The personality of the artist, at first a cry or a cadence or a mood and then a fluid and lambent narrative, finally refines itself out of existence, impersonalises itself (Joyce 2000: 180-181). Also in *The Oxford Handbook of Aesthetics* aesthetic experience is defined as "disinterestedness, or detachment from desires, needs and practical concerns" (Levinson 2003: 6). Gabriel seems to be on course to becoming an artist finally. The experience of detachedness from his feelings moreover creates a sudden and intense awareness of transience:

> Poor Aunt Julia! She, too, would soon be a shade [...] Soon, perhaps, he would be sitting in that same drawing-room, dressed in black, his silk hat on his knees. The blinds would be drawn down and Aunt Kate would be sitting beside him, crying and blowing her nose and telling him how Julia had died (Joyce 1971: 55).

He reflects about his insufficient ability to express what he feels once more: "He would cast about in his mind for some words that might console her, and would find only lame and useless ones. Yes, yes: that would happen very soon" (Joyce 1971: 55). After this anticipation Gabriel also ponders the best way to dismiss life, comparing Michael Furey's death to the passing of the moribund party guests: "One by one, they were all becoming shades. Better pass boldly into that other world, in the full glory of some passion, than fade and wither dismally with age" (Joyce 1971: 56). This intense reflection about evanescence induces Gabriel to empathize with the dead coming as close to a state of death himself as probably possible:

> Other forms were near. His soul had approached that region where dwell the vast hosts of the dead. He was conscious of, but could not apprehend, their wayward and flickering existence. His own identity was fading out into a grey impalpable world: the solid world itself, which these dead had one time reared and lived in, was dissolving and dwindling. (Joyce 1971: 56)

This corresponds to a near death experience wherein Gabriel, who had only just become aware of his rather unpleasant identity, loses it again already. According to Rupp this scene "reflects the sense of dissolution of the self that characterizes both the insane and the mystical" (Rupp 2010: 5). But Joyce even admitted himself in his conversations with Arthur Power that "[i]n fact all great men have had that vein [of madness] in them; it was the source of their greatness; the reasonable man achieves nothing" (Power 1974: 60). Gabriel appearing reasonable and sophisticated at the beginning can only become a poet by facing the abyss and embarking on the evanescence of life. This development of Gabriel's personality is also represented in the changing of the semantics he attributes to the snow. The "intermittent (and emblematic) snowfall" (Doloff 2008: 483) at the beginning of the short story is described rather playful causing a "light fringe [...] like a cape on the shoulders of his overcoat and [...] toecaps on the toes of his goloshes" (Joyce 1971: 9). During the course of the night however after Gabriel's extra-terrestrial epiphany he perceives the snow as highly symbolic for death: "Snow has thus undergone a symbolic change in Gabriel's mind, from a way of representing his desire for escape into an idealized urban landscape to a representation of the ultimate escape of death" (Morrissey 1988: 28). Or to put it in other words: the story "ends with the universal interment of corpses under the blanket of snow" (Merino 2016: 135), the snow silences any sound and equalizes everything by dissolving differences and identity:

> It had begun to snow again. He watched sleepily the flakes, silver and dark, falling obliquely against the lamplight. [...] It was falling on every part of the dark central plain, on the treeless hills, falling softly upon the Bog of Allen and, farther westward, softly falling into the dark mutinous Shannon waves. It was falling, too, upon every part of the lonely churchyard on the hill where Michael Furey lay buried. It lay thickly drifted on the crooked crosses and headstones, on the spears of the little gate, on the barren thorns. His soul swooned slowly as he heard the snow falling faintly through the universe and faintly falling, like the descent of their last end, upon all the living and the dead. (Joyce 1971: 56)

This last passage sounds almost musical in its rhythmic flow even enforced by the multitude of stylistic means like alliterations, inversions, similes and enumerations, all together creating the impression of a paradoxically reassuring equality between life and death. "The initially sharp distinction between past and present is transcended at the narrative climax in an epiphanic moment of temporal simultaneity and dissolves, at the end, in a unifying cosmic vision" (Caporaletti 1997: 410). Gabriel's preceding self becomes insignificant in the last scene of the short story. "In these piercing images and hard-edged sounds, Gabriel's mind is penetrated as it has not yet been by an experience of loss, of the world outside himself, of the finality of death" (Jones 2000: 115). And yet Gabriel is not defeated by death in the end: "death is but a preliminary--if necessary--stage in the movement toward rebirth" (Anspaugh 1994: 5). He is reborn as an artist as this lyrical and profound insight shows. Murphy claims that Gabriel "can never illuminate [...] his consciousness via some epiphany" (Murphy 2004: 471). And also Bazargan states that Gabriel "who matures during the course of an evening [...], finally fails to achieve an authentic transformation" (Bazargan 2004: 52) without delivering any justification. Nonetheless I would rather affiliate to Munich who describes this phenomenon as artistic conversion: "an essential alteration in the nature of the writer, serves to confirm the death. The convert turns away from his old beliefs and, by repudiating that past, asserts that he is a new, that is, a different, person" (Munich 1984: 174). Taking this into consideration, Gabriel resembles Stephen in *A Portrait of the Artist as a Young Man* once again who is humiliated at the beginning of every chapter and always gains a sort of triumph resulting in strength, pride and self-consciousness and finally in becoming an artist. Gabriel also transmigrates an extreme development and finally accomplishes his poetic style in adopting an artist's aesthetic attitude towards life and death at the end. "The poet is thus the one who, in a moment of grace, discovers the profound soul of things [...] Epiphany is thus a way of discovering reality (Eco 2007: 344).

6. Conclusion

It is remarkable how many allusions to death are contained in James Joyce's short story *The Dead* although seeming inappropriate in the context of an annual dance. Nonetheless these omnipresent gloomy references provide a framework which casts the story in a whole other light and sensitizes for the subject of mortality. Additionally the fact that Gabriel often is the one who brings in the moribund topics already hints on his willingness to face death which manifests especially at the end of the story. In the following the reader's attention is drawn to Gabriel's restlessness, his lack of self-assurance and of the ability of expressing himself properly. He has obviously not yet been arrived in his life, is caught up in his emotions and is yearning for distance towards others and also towards his inner world. Nonetheless many allusions to Stephen in *A Portrait of the Artist as a Young Man* already show, that Gabriel might have the requirements for creating poetry. After the turning point Gabriel is inspired by love and lust but he is still longing for escape which he cannot achieve yet. Not until being challenged by the dead after Gretta's shocking revelation he finally reaches comprehensive detachedness in a form of emotional catharsis by coming as close to death as possible. But instead of being defeated, Gabriel is rather reborn into an artist. He obtains an epiphany revealing reality in the poetical last paragraph, full of rhythm and stylistic devices. The changing in the semantics he attributes to the snow which becomes a symbol for mortality exemplifies the development of Gabriel's aesthetic outlook on life and death. "Regardless of our specific interpretation of Gabriel's psyche, I would like to argue that the story's conclusion evokes a distinct sense of poeticity, a feeling that transcends a regular, 'prosaic' mode of narration" (Fishelov 2013/2014: 265). Taking everything into consideration it can be asserted that the initial thesis that Gabriel turns into an artist by facing death proves well-founded.

References

Primary Sources

Joyce, J. 1971. *The Dead*. Ed. W. Spiegelberg. München.

Joyce, J. 2000. *A Portrait of the Artist as a Young Man*. Ed. J. Johnson. Oxford University Press.

Levinson, J. 2003. "Philosophical Aesthetics: An Overview". *The Oxford Handbook of Aesthetics*. Ed. J. Levinson. Oxford University Press: 3-24.

Ovid. 2011. *Metamorphosen*. Ed. H. Breitenbach. Stuttgart.

Power, A. 1974. *Conversations with James Joyce*. Ed. C. Hart. London.

Secondary Sources

Anspaugh, K. 1994. "'Three mortal hour(i)s': Female gothic in Joyce's 'The Dead'". *Studies in Short Fiction* 31.1: 1-11.

Bazargan, S. 2004. "Epiphany as Scene of Performance". *A New & Complex Sensation. Essays on Joyce's Dubliners*. Ed. O. Frawley. Dublin. 44-54.

Benbida, H. 2013. "Gabriel Conroy as a Concept of James Joyce's Personality in The Dead". Unpubl. PhD dissertation, Kadi Merbah University Ouargla.

Caporaletti, S. 1997. "The Thematization of Time in E. M. Forster's 'The Eternal Moment' and Joyce's 'The Dead'". *Twentieth Century Literature* 43.4: 406-419.

Doloff, S. 2008. Snowy Revelations: a Possible Inspiration for the Ending of James Joyce's 'The Dead' in Dostoevsky's Notes from the Underground. *Notes and Queries*: 483-485.

Eco, U. 2007. "The Artist and Medieval Thought in the Early Joyce". *A Portrait of the Artist as a Young Man*. Ed. J. P. Riquelme. New York. 329-348.

Fishelov, D. 2013/2014. "Poetry and Poeticity in Joyce's 'The Dead,' Baudelaire's *Le Spleen de Paris*, and Yehuda Amichai". *Connotations* 23.2: 261-282.

Jones, A. 2000. "Bringing 'The Dead' to Life: Reading James Joyce". *Journal of Applied Psychoanalytic Studies* 2: 109-115.

Loomis, C. C. Jr. 1960. "Structure and Sympathy in Joyce's 'The Dead'". *Modern Language Association* 75.1: 149-151.

Merino, J. Á. O. 2016. "A 'Distant Music': Invoking Phantasmagoria in Joyce's 'The Dead'". *Estudios Irlandeses* 11: 132-148.

Morrissey, L. J. 1988. "Inner and Outer Perceptions in Joyce's 'The Dead'". *Studies in Short Fiction* 25.1: 21-29.

Munich, A. A. 1984. "Form and Subtext in Joyce's 'The Dead'". *Modern Philology* 82.2: 173-184.

Murphy, S. P. 1995. "Passing Boldly into That Other World of (W)Holes: Narrativity and Subjectivity in James Joyce's 'The Dead'". *Studies in Short Fiction* 32.3: 463-474.

Norris, M. 1989. "Stifled Back Answers: The Gender Politics of Art in Joyce's 'The Dead'". *Modern Fiction Studies* 35.5: 479-503.

Rupp, G. V. 2010. "Self Enlightenment in Woolf, Joyce, and Nietzsche". *Comparative Literature and Culture* 12.3: 1-8.

Winston, G. C. 2004. "Militarism and 'The Dead'". *A New & Complex Sensation. Essays on Joyce's Dubliners.* Ed. O. Frawley. Dublin. 122-132.

YOUR KNOWLEDGE HAS VALUE

- We will publish your bachelor's and master's thesis, essays and papers

- Your own eBook and book - sold worldwide in all relevant shops

- Earn money with each sale

Upload your text at www.GRIN.com
and publish for free

www.ingramcontent.com/pod-product-compliance
Lightning Source LLC
LaVergne TN
LVHW092103060526
838201LV00047B/1549